Original title:
The Structure of Verse

Copyright © 2024 Creative Arts Management OÜ
All rights reserved.

Author: Thor Castlebury
ISBN HARDBACK: 978-9916-88-052-4
ISBN PAPERBACK: 978-9916-88-053-1

Vibrations of Verse

Words dance lightly in the air,
Echoes linger without a care.
Rhythms pulse through heart and mind,
In every line, new worlds we find.

Soft whispers weave from pen to page,
Each letter turned, a silent sage.
Feeling's current, strong and true,
In this flow, we are renewed.

Verses rise like morning light,
Chasing shadows, taking flight.
In the silence, our thoughts speak,
Each stroke of ink, a bond unique.

Together, melodies align,
In every stanza, life does shine.
So let us sing, let us write,
In vibrations, we ignite.

The Craft of Connection

Hands create the stories told,
In simple lines, our hearts unfold.
Bridges built on verbal streams,
In each encounter, hope redeems.

Fingers trace the paths of thought,
Moments seized and feelings caught.
With every word, a spark ignites,
Connecting souls through darkened nights.

Threads of meaning intertwine,
In the fabric, love will shine.
Crafting bonds that time won't sever,
Together we stand, now and forever.

Let voices blend in sweet refrain,
Through laughter, joy, and even pain.
The craft we cherish, ever grand,
In this connection, hand in hand.

Verses in Architecture

In shadows cast by stone and beam,
Vertical lines that touch the dream.
Windows whisper stories told,
Framed in history, bold and old.

Arches rise like waves in flight,
Balconies cradle day and night.
Columns stand with silent grace,
Holding up this timeless space.

Rhythms and Rhyme

In the pulse of words, we find our way,
Each syllable dances, come what may.
A heartbeat felt in verse so sweet,
Melodies form where thoughts and dreams meet.

The music swells with every line,
Bringing life to thoughts divine.
Echoes linger in the air,
Whispers of poets, a shared prayer.

Cadence of Creation

Brush strokes blend where colors play,
On canvas bright, emotions sway.
Clay molds under gentle hands,
Crafting dreams from Earth's commands.

In sculpted forms, our visions rise,
A dance of light beneath open skies.
Each gesture speaks, each detail sings,
Creation breathes in sacred things.

Frameworks of Emotion

Within the heart, a structure stands,
Supporting hopes in gentle hands.
Walls of trust and windows wide,
Open spaces where love resides.

Pain and joy in every beam,
Building bridges, breaking seams.
In this fortress, we find peace,
Emotions framed, never cease.

The Architecture of Rhyme

In shadows cast by whispered words,
A dance of thoughts, like singing birds.
With bricks of syllables, we build
A realm where dreams are gently thrilled.

The arches curve in rhythmic flow,
Each line, a path where feelings grow.
Columns strong of meaning stand,
Holding close the hearts of man.

Verses in Harmony

Together we create a song,
Where every note invites us long.
In unity, our voices blend,
A melody that won't descend.

Each word we share is stitched with care,
A tapestry that we all share.
Chords of laughter, whispers soft,
In harmony, our spirits loft.

Foundations of Expression

Laying stones of pure intent,
Crafting thoughts that help us vent.
With colors bright, we paint the sky,
In the art of words, we learn to fly.

Each layer builds a deeper truth,
A quest that spans from age to youth.
Foundations strong, we rise above,
In the cradle of shared love.

The Tapestry of Thought

Threads of wisdom woven tight,
In patterns rich, a world ignites.
Colors swirl, entwined they dance,
Creating forms from every chance.

With every stitch, new visions arise,
A canvas wide beneath the skies.
In this weave, our secrets blend,
A story penned that knows no end.

Currents of Composition

Words flow like water, soft and clear,
Carving the landscape of what we hear.
In whispers they gather, in waves they rise,
Painting visions beneath endless skies.

Each thought a ripple, expanding in space,
A journey of meaning, each line finds its place.
The current may twist, the direction may bend,
Yet the heart of the matter shall never suspend.

Signposts of Sentiment

Emotions are markers along our way,
Guiding us gently when words start to sway.
In laughter and sorrow, in joy and in pain,
The signposts stand tall, both sturdy and plain.

They lead us through valleys, they lift us on high,
Reminders that feelings are not passed by.
Each sign a reflection of tales to unfold,
Mapping our journeys in stories retold.

Mosaic of Metaphors

Shards of meaning, arranged with intent,
Creating a picture where feelings are bent.
Each piece a story, a glimpse of the whole,
Crafting connections that deepen the soul.

Colors of language blend rich and bright,
Illuminating truths in the softest light.
A tapestry woven of wisdom and art,
Each metaphor whispers, igniting the heart.

The Fabric of Feeling

Threads of emotion, entwined in a weave,
Stitching together what we dare to believe.
The fabric is strong, yet delicate too,
Each pattern a story, in shades of the blue.

Sewn with intention, the fabric unfolds,
A blanket of solace, a warmth that upholds.
In each vibrant fiber, a narrative lies,
The fabric of feeling, where truth never dies.

Verse in Motion

The winds whisper softly to the trees,
Leaves dance lightly, caught in the breeze.
Words flow like rivers, swift and bright,
Each line a step in the silent night.

With every heartbeat, the rhythm grows,
A journey unfolds where the spirit flows.
Chasing shadows under the pale moon,
Time may be fleeting, but dreams stay in tune.

Soul of the Stanza

In each heartbeat, a story unfurls,
A tapestry woven with thoughts and swirls.
Whispers of hope in a silent gaze,
Captured in moments, a timeless phase.

The essence of language, both fierce and mild,
Each verse a canvas, a soul of a child.
Words wrap around us, a warm embrace,
In the depth of the stanza, we find our place.

Divisions of Delight

Joy is scattered like stars in the sky,
Each twinkle a promise, a sweet lullaby.
With laughter, we paint the spaces between,
In the palette of life, we craft our scene.

Moments of bliss, like petals in bloom,
Brighten the corners of a shadowed room.
Divided by sorrow, united by grace,
We gather the light in every warm space.

Guiding Rhythms

Upon the beat of our heart's true song,
We find the strength to carry us along.
The cadence will lead us through night and day,
In harmony's arms, we willingly sway.

Each note is a whisper, a guiding light,
Filling the canvas of the darkest night.
With passion igniting the steps that we take,
In the dance of the beats, we awaken, we wake.

Patterns in the Air

Waves of color dance and sway,
Tracing paths in bright display.
Whispers carried through the breeze,
Patterns written in the leaves.

Clouds like ink on azure skies,
Creating tales that mesmerize.
Shapes that shift and intertwine,
Nature's art, a grand design.

Moments pause to take it in,
As shadows flicker under skin.
A harmony of light and dark,
The fleeting beauty leaves a mark.

In every twist, a story spun,
In every sigh, a journey begun.
Patterns spiral, ebb and flow,
In the air, a world to know.

Echoes of Form

Shapes emerge from silence deep,
Molding thoughts we dare to keep.
In the void, a voice will call,
Echoes bound to rise and fall.

Lines converge, and curves align,
Carving paths that intertwine.
In shadows, truth begins to speak,
Crafting forms that feel unique.

Mirrors reflect what we can see,
In the stillness, we find free.
A resonance that grips the heart,
Echoes linger, never part.

Within each shape, a world resides,
In every turn, a journey hides.
Echoing in vibrant hue,
Forms of life in every view.

Shapes of Sound

Melodies that sway and glide,
In the air, they twist and slide.
Rhythms pulse, a vibrant flow,
Shapes of sound that rise and grow.

Harmony in every beat,
Echoing in time, so sweet.
Voices blend, create a song,
In this dance, we all belong.

Strings that hum a soft refrain,
Percussion echoes like the rain.
In every note, a story told,
Shapes of sound, a warmth in cold.

Resonance crafting space and time,
A symphony, profound and prime.
In the silence, hear the spark,
Forms and figures in the dark.

Inks and Measures

Droplets fall like graceful grace,
Inks that paint each word and space.
Lines defined with every stroke,
Measures blend until they choke.

Papers whisper, tales unfold,
Stories captured from the bold.
In each margin, life depicted,
All the moments interdictive.

Pens that dance upon the sheet,
Marking time in rhythm's beat.
Each measure, a heartbeat pressed,
Inks and dreams now manifest.

Crafting realms from thought and ink,
Inviting hearts and minds to think.
In every mark, a universe,
Written deep, our souls disperse.

Light and Shadow in Lines

In the dawn's gentle glow,
Shadows stretch and recede,
Lines of light dance and play,
A symphony of deeds.

Beneath the whispering trees,
Shadows hide in embrace,
Sunlit paths shift and weave,
An intricate lace.

On canvas of the sky,
Clouds drift, old tales unwind,
Light reveals hidden dreams,
While shadows remain blind.

In the twilight's soft hush,
Lines blur in sweet retreat,
Both light and shadow meet,
In harmony, they're sweet.

Enigmas of Structure

Within the walls' firm grasp,
Mystery coins its own fate,
Shapes whisper secrets low,
As minds recalibrate.

Symmetry holds its breath,
Angles sharp and refined,
In corners, echoes linger,
In shadows, truth is blind.

Patterns weave through the air,
Crafting stories untold,
In spaces carved by time,
Where warmth meets the cold.

Beneath the clamor of life,
Order breeds chaos anew,
Enigmas take their stand,
In every wall we construe.

Threads of Tradition

In the loom of the old world,
Threads intertwine with care,
History casts its net,
In wisdom that we share.

Voices of those before,
Resonate in the weave,
Stitch by stitch, we connect,
Patterns we can't perceive.

Tales from distant shores,
Whispered in every loop,
Binding generations,
In a vibrant group.

As time comes to a close,
In fabric we find our way,
Threads of tradition bind,
In each new bright array.

The Weave of Words

In the tapestry of thought,
Words spin soft and bright,
Each sentence a new thread,
Woven with pure delight.

Metaphors dance like flames,
Similes twirl with grace,
In every written line,
We find our sacred space.

Stories blend and collide,
Imaginations soar,
In the weave of our words,
We unlock the door.

As the pages turn,
A universe unfurls,
In the fabric of language,
A world full of pearls.

Cadences and Constructs

In rhythm profound, we find our way,
With beats that guide, come what may.
In whispers soft, the echoes sing,
Each note, a moment, threaded string.

The structure holds, a dance of thought,
In every line, a lesson taught.
With metaphors dressed in vibrant hue,
The canvas blooms with visions new.

Through measured steps, we trace the lines,
In symphonies where silence shines.
Constructs rise from ashes past,
Each voice a dream, each memory cast.

From chaos born, a song takes flight,
In every shadow, we find the light.
Cadences entwined in timeless ways,
Life's melody, a weave that sways.

Weaving Words

In fabric rich and colors bright,
We stitch our tales into the night.
With fibers twined and thoughts unfurled,
A tapestry of words is swirled.

Each thread a whisper, soft and clear,
In verses shared, we hold them near.
We spin the stories, round and round,
In every heartbeat, life is found.

From needle's point, intentions flow,
In patterns bold, our dreams will grow.
A quilt of voices, patchwork heart,
Each piece a memory, each seam a part.

Weaving words like strands of fate,
In every silence, we resonate.
A craft of love, with joy bestowed,
In every tale, a path is road.

Arches of Alliteration

Beneath the arches, words align,
A dance of sounds, a twist divine.
With playful tunes, the voices play,
In echoes bright, they find their way.

Soft whispers weave in shadowed light,
Each syllable, a bird in flight.
In alliteration's sweet embrace,
We find the music, find our place.

Curved and flowing, like a stream,
The rhythm sings, a shared dream.
Through consonants that cling and coo,
The art of sounds brings forth the new.

With every echo, stories twine,
In arches strong, our lives entwine.
Let us rejoice in sounds so true,
In alliteration's dance, me and you.

Frameworks of Fancy

In structures bold, our dreams take shape,
With fantasy's wings, we softly scrape.
Each corner turned, a new design,
In buildings bright, our hopes align.

From arches high to windows wide,
In every space, our thoughts abide.
With colors swirled and visions grand,
We sketch the dreams with heart and hand.

Through doorways leading far and near,
In frameworks built, we hold what's dear.
With fanciful thoughts, we weave and mold,
In every layer, stories told.

Let hearts be light, let spirits soar,
In frameworks of fancy, we explore.
With every laugh and whispered line,
We carve a world, forever mine.

Echoing Essentials

Whispers float in the air,
Carried softly by the breeze,
Moments linger, rare and fair,
Echoes dance among the trees.

Sunlight kisses the ground,
Nature hums a timeless tune,
In each shadow, life is found,
Beneath the watchful moon.

Colors blend and fade away,
Brushstrokes on a canvas bright,
All our dreams wish to convey,
Living stories take their flight.

In the heart of every sound,
Resonance of life unfolds,
Echoing the joy we've ground,
In the silence, warmth beholds.

The Pulse of Poetry

Words like rivers, flowing free,
Capturing thoughts we hold dear,
Each heartbeat a melody,
Poetry whispers in our ear.

Verses rise like tides at night,
Dancing under starlit skies,
In each line, a spark of light,
Illuminating hidden highs.

Rhythms pulse within our veins,
Rhyme and reason intertwine,
In the chaos, beauty reigns,
Crafting dreams through every line.

Feel the cadence, sense the flow,
With each stanza, we ignite,
The essence in the words we sow,
Binding hearts with pure delight.

Sculpture of Sentences

Chiseled words, a form takes shape,
Crafted with care, a timeless art,
Every phrase learns to escape,
From the silence, it imparts.

Lines curve gently, shadows cast,
In the thoughts that dare to breathe,
Each emotion, tightly fast,
Carved by dreams that we believe.

Polished surfaces reflect light,
Honest truths held in each line,
Sculpted voices, bold and bright,
A dance of meaning, pure design.

In this gallery of our mind,
Sentences breathe in sculpted grace,
Echoes of the thoughts we find,
A masterpiece in quiet space.

The Flow of Fragments

Scattered pieces, lost and found,
Ripples in an endless sea,
Each fragment waits, a voice unbound,
Yearning for a place to be.

Moments captured, brief yet deep,
Floating softly in the night,
As memories awaken sleep,
In their whisper, a source of light.

Collage of dreams that intertwine,
Every shard a story tells,
In the chaos, patterns shine,
Like the ringing of lost bells.

Flowing gently, time reveals,
What was hidden in the stream,
Fragments dance, the heart appeals,
In their rhythm, we can dream.

Lines that Build Dreams

With every stroke, we sketch our fate,
Colors blend, hearts resonate.
Hopes take flight like birds on high,
Chasing shadows in the sky.

Each thread we weave in gentle care,
Lays a path through burdens bare.
Dreams take root in fertile ground,
Where whispers of tomorrow sound.

We raise the walls with stories told,
Crafting futures, brave and bold.
A ladder of faith we climb with grace,
Seeking stars in endless space.

Lines connect in perfect form,
Creating warmth, a shelter warm.
In every curve, our hopes reside,
A tapestry where dreams abide.

Patterns in Stanza

In the rhythm, secrets lie,
Echoes of a silent sigh.
Verses dance in graceful arcs,
Telling tales of unseen sparks.

Patterns twist like vines that climb,
Interwoven threads of time.
Stanzas build a bridge of thought,
Connecting hearts with love, unbought.

Each line a note in harmony,
Crafting paths for you and me.
A symphony of woven words,
Awakening the dreams unheard.

In the quiet, meaning blooms,
Through the echoes, life resumes.
Patterns glow in moonlit grace,
Every stanza finds its place.

Foundations of Metaphor

In the depth of language, layers grow,
Foundations built where meanings flow.
Metaphors stand tall and wise,
Reflecting truths in bright disguise.

Each phrase a stone, set with care,
Upon these pillars, thoughts ensnare.
Images rise like towers high,
Bridging realms where dreams can fly.

The heart of words, a silent plea,
To build a world where we are free.
Foundations firm, yet light as air,
Metaphors that lead us there.

Through language we can shape the light,
Illuminating dark, with bright.
In every metaphor, a spark,
Guiding us through the deep and dark.

The Blueprint of Breath

Every breath, a silent song,
Carving paths where we belong.
Waves of air, in gentle flow,
Source of life, in ebb and glow.

The blueprint drawn in nascent sighs,
Where aspirations rise and fly.
Inhaling dreams, exhaling fears,
Tracing hopes with flowing tears.

With every pulse, we paint our way,
Crafting lives in the light of day.
Breath by breath, we build anew,
A canvas bright, a vibrant hue.

From whispered thoughts to roaring cheers,
In every breath, our story steers.
The blueprint of life unfolds with grace,
A journey marked by time and space.

Illustrations in Ink

In shadows deep, the stories lie,
With every stroke, the dreams can fly.
A world unfolds on pages bright,
Ink weaves tales in black and white.

Lines that dance with whispers soft,
Create a realm both lost and oft.
Each mark a brush with hidden fate,
A canvas wide, we contemplate.

Characters breathe, passions ignite,
In every corner, a new delight.
The ink runs wild, like rivers flow,
Painting emotions we all know.

From silence, sound begins to play,
In every hue, the heart will sway.
With illustrations rich and bold,
A world through ink begins to unfold.

The Cascade of Cadence

A rhythm plays, the night awakes,
With echoes soft, the silence breaks.
Notes that dance in twilight's glow,
In waves of sound, our spirits flow.

The heartbeats sync to nature's song,
In harmony where we belong.
Each whisper winds through trees so high,
A melody beneath the sky.

With gusts that sweep, the leaves they sway,
In cadence bright, they join the play.
A symphony of life be sung,
In every breath, the world is young.

As stars align, the music swells,
In twinkling lights, the magic dwells.
A cascade rich, a tune divine,
In every note, our souls entwine.

Fleeting Frames of Thoughts

A whisper drifts like autumn leaves,
In mind's embrace, the spirit weaves.
Moments captured, flickers bright,
In frames of thought, we find our light.

Ephemeral, they gently pass,
Like shadows cast on blades of grass.
With tender care, we hold them near,
These fleeting frames, so held in cheer.

Each thought a spark, a blaze of dreams,
In silver streams where longing gleams.
We chase the sunsets, watch them fade,
In precious thoughts, our hearts cascade.

So let them flow, these thoughts in time,
A dance of words that plays sublime.
In fleeting frames, our stories blend,
A tapestry that knows no end.

Footprints of the Muse

In the silence, whispers call,
Footprints left, where shadows fall.
The muse will walk a winding way,
In every step, the heart will sway.

Through tangled paths of dreams unbeheld,
In secret places, stories swelled.
Each footfall marks a tale to share,
In hidden corners, she leaves her air.

With fleeting grace, she brings the light,
In darkest hours, a spark ignites.
Through realms of wonder, bold and true,
The muse will guide, revealing new.

So wander forth, and trace her line,
In every moment, let your soul shine.
For footprints left, a path to muse,
In every heart, her charm we choose.

The Geometry of Rhythm

In circles round the sun's embrace,
The beats align in perfect space.
Angles dance with subtle grace,
Each pulse a map, a measured trace.

Lines converge and drift apart,
Echoed whispers, a silent art.
Patterns carve the soul's own chart,
In every sound, the mind's restart.

Symmetry in every note,
Melodies that gently float.
Each rhythm strikes a hopeful quote,
An ordered heart, a vibrant boat.

In harmony, we find our way,
Through every dusk, through every day.
The geometry that guides our play,
In beats and bars, we choose to stay.

Lyrical Landscapes

Mountains rise with tales so grand,
Whispers of the earth and sand.
Each valley sings a soft command,
In lyrical swells, we understand.

Rivers flow with silver light,
Bridges built from dreams in flight.
Across the hills, the stars ignite,
In every shadow, hope burns bright.

Fields of flowers, wild and free,
A tapestry for all to see.
Nature's verses call to thee,
In every petal, harmony.

The skies alight with colors bold,
Stories in the clouds unfold.
The landscapes rich, a treasure told,
In every moment, beauty's gold.

Harmonies in Design

Lines and shapes in perfect blend,
Crafted tales that never end.
In each detail, messages send,
A symphony on which we depend.

Colors clash and softly meet,
Creating worlds beneath our feet.
Patterns pulse with a vibrant beat,
In every frame, the heart's own heat.

Textures weave a story rare,
With every layer, love and care.
In designs that boldly dare,
A dance of forms, a silent flare.

In art we find our vast expanse,
Where dreams and visions twist and dance.
Through harmonies, we take a chance,
In every stroke, a lasting trance.

The Fabric of Feeling

Threads of warmth and woven grace,
Each emotion finds its place.
In every stitch, a soft embrace,
The fabric wraps, time can't erase.

Colors bleed into the night,
Tales of joy and sorrow's light.
We wear our hearts in pure delight,
In every fold, a deeper sight.

Textures whisper secrets shared,
In every layer, souls are bared.
Moments stitched with love and care,
The fabric holds what we have dared.

Through patterns, we begin to see,
The tapestry of you and me.
In woven dreams, we are set free,
In every thread, our memory.

Cadence and Composition

In whispers soft, the notes align,
A rhythm born from dusk to shine.
The sound of hearts in harmony,
Each pulse a perfect symphony.

With ink that flows like rivers wide,
They dance upon the page, with pride.
Each word a step, each line a glide,
In time's embrace, our thoughts reside.

From silence springs a vibrant tune,
Where shadows meet the light of noon.
In every breath, a verse unfolds,
A story penned, a dream retold.

So let us sing, and let us write,
In cadence bold, through day and night.
For every soul has tales to share,
In whispered words, an art laid bare.

The Geometry of Stanzas

In corners sharp, the lines converge,
A pattern born from thought's emerge.
With angles keen, we draw the frame,
Each stanza holds a spark of flame.

The circles round, they weave and twine,
In shapes poetic, hearts entwine.
Each measure counts, each beat in time,
As voices rise, through prose we climb.

From squares of thought to arcs of dreams,
The fabric bends; the essence gleams.
In every shape, a tale resides,
The geometry of hearts, that guides.

So let us sketch with vivid words,
A map of feelings, softly stirred.
In every stanza, life defined,
The geometry of hearts combined.

Weaving Words Together

With threads of thought, we spin and weave,
In tapestries of tales, believe.
Each fiber strong, each color bright,
The fabric holds our dreams in sight.

From silken whispers to sturdy yarn,
We craft a world from dusk till dawn.
The loom of time, it hums a tune,
As sentences and stanzas bloom.

Interlaced paths where stories flow,
In every knot, the memories grow.
With hands of grace, we craft the seam,
A quilt of hopes, a woven dream.

So gather round, let's share the cloth,
In every thread, our hearts betroth.
For words can weave a life anew,
In fabric rich, our souls break through.

Frameworks of Emotion

In blueprints drawn, our hearts take flight,
The frames of dreams built through the night.
With beams of joy and walls of fear,
We craft the spaces, hold them dear.

Each window high reflects our truth,
A glimpse of hope, the essence of youth.
With doors ajar, we welcome light,
In every corner, love ignites.

Foundations strong, in laughter's tone,
We build a world that feels like home.
The structure bends with every sigh,
As walls embrace the low and high.

So let's construct with heart and mind,
A framework where our souls can bind.
In every corner, joy shall dwell,
A testament of love to tell.

Tidal Waves of Tone

Waves crash with a roaring sound,
Echoes dance on shores unbound.
Each note flows like sea and foam,
In harmony, we find our home.

Riding rhythms, hearts will sway,
Pulling us in, then away.
Melodies like tides do play,
In the night, they softly stay.

Crescendo builds, a powerful force,
Crashing on our inner source.
The ebb and flow, a calming grace,
In the sound, we find our place.

Let the waves of tone embrace,
Washing worries, leaving space.
Feel the rhythm, let it be,
In the waves, we feel so free.

The Lattice of Language

Words interwoven, threads of thought,
In every sentence, battles fought.
Crafting meaning, a delicate art,
Each verse a canvas, a brand new start.

In whispers soft, the stories swell,
Through twilight's veil, they start to tell.
Symbols dance, connect the lines,
In every pause, the heart inclines.

Letters link in a vibrant mesh,
Creating worlds, our minds refresh.
In the lattice, ideas blend,
A tapestry of messages to send.

So let us weave, each thread, each tone,
In the lattice, never alone.
With every word, we paint the skies,
A universe where meaning lies.

Sketching with Sound

In the quiet, whispers draw,
Sketches form without a flaw.
Notes take shape on canvas bare,
Filling space with vibrant air.

Brush of rhythms, strokes of grace,
Each melody seeks its place.
Colors blend in harmonies bright,
Curves of sound in soft twilight.

Sculpting silence into song,
Where we feel we do belong.
Sketching dreams with every beat,
In each chorus, we are fleet.

Let your spirit find the tune,
Dance with shadows beneath the moon.
In this art, let love abound,
As we go on, sketching sound.

A Symphony of Stanzas

In the heart of every line,
Melodies and meanings shine.
Stanzas weave a careful thread,
In the silence, dreams are fed.

Chords of language, bold and bright,
Echo gently through the night.
Each phrase dances, takes its flight,
In the symphony of light.

A chorus formed from whispered thoughts,
Binding truths, connecting dots.
In the rhythm, we find our way,
Through darkened skies to brighter day.

Let the music guide our words,
In the stillness, truth is heard.
Together we create and play,
In this symphony, we sway.

Experiments in Expression

Words collide in vibrant air,
Colors dance, a bold affair.
Thoughts unleashed, no chains to bind,
Echoes linger, free the mind.

Brushes flick and colors blend,
Canvas waits for dreams to send.
Life's a swirl, a vibrant stream,
Each stroke whispers, each a dream.

Voices rise, a chorus strong,
In this space, we all belong.
Rhythms pulse, a heartbeat's call,
In expression, we stand tall.

Joys and sorrows, hand in hand,
Together we will take a stand.
Art reveals what words can't say,
In our hearts, it finds its way.

Shapes of Silence

In stillness, shadows softly creep,
Whispers echo, secrets keep.
Contours blend, a silent space,
In every pause, we find our grace.

Void of noise, yet thick with thought,
In quietude, our souls are caught.
Fingers trace the lines of air,
Holding close what's barely there.

Time suspend, the world awash,
In this moment, feelings posh.
Every breath, a prayer, a sigh,
In the silence, dreams can fly.

Dancing shadows in dim-lit halls,
The heart listens, the spirit calls.
In the hush, we find the light,
Shapes of silence, soft and bright.

The Flowing Framework

Rivers carve their ancient paths,
Nature's brush, in subtle swaths.
Structure built from elements,
Flowing freely, consequence.

Beneath the surface, life abounds,
In every curve, a world surrounds.
Flexibility in solid form,
In flowing frameworks, we transform.

Roots entwined beneath the stone,
In every growth, the seed is sown.
Life evolves through twists and bends,
An endless cycle that transcends.

Merging worlds of earth and sky,
Together we will soar and fly.
In this dance, each part belongs,
A silent hymn, a muted song.

Patterns of Persistence

In every struggle, strength is found,
Through winding roads, we are unbound.
Step by step, we hold the flame,
In the face of doubt, we claim.

Every challenge shapes our core,
Through the tempest, we explore.
Resilience weaves the thread of fate,
In patterns rich, we cultivate.

Time unfurls, a tapestry,
Stitches made of you and me.
In the loom, our stories blend,
Together, start and never end.

Drawing strength from what we face,
In the struggle, we find grace.
Persistent hearts, we'll stand our ground,
In unity, our hope is found.

Intonations of Intellect

Thoughts swirl like autumn leaves,
In quiet corners of the mind.
Whispers echo truths untold,
In shadows where the bright thoughts bind.

Riddles dance in flickering light,
Each question a step into the dark.
Logic weaves a tapestry tight,
Unraveling threads, igniting the spark.

Beyond boundaries, ideas soar,
On wings of reason, bold and free.
A journey through the mental door,
Where wisdom blooms like ancient trees.

Embrace the elegance of thought,
In its depth, both rich and rare.
Discover what the mind has sought,
In the maze of what we dare.

Crafting Cadences

In rhythmic beats, the heart aligns,
With stories woven, soft and clear.
Every note a bridge that binds,
   Turning silence into cheer.

Words like rivers gently flow,
Carving paths through timeless hills.
Echoing whispers from below,
Where every voice the spirit fills.

Melodies wrapped in tender grace,
Dance like shadows in the breeze.
Each cadence finds its rightful place,
   Bringing solace, granting ease.

Together, they create a song,
A tapestry of sound and rhyme.
In this harmony, we belong,
As echoes stretch beyond all time.

Tones and Textures

Colors blend beneath the skin,
Layers whisper stories old.
Textures tell where dreams have been,
In every crease, a truth unfolds.

The brush strokes soft, the canvas wide,
Each hue a heartbeat, bold and bright.
In shadows deep, the secrets hide,
Awaiting dawn's revealing light.

A symphony of senses play,
Inviting eyes to linger long.
In every shade, a wordless say,
Where silence blooms and thoughts belong.

Artistry in every breath,
Crafted deftly, soft, yet strong.
In tones that dance, defy the death,
Of moments grasped in fleeting song.

Portraits of Prose

In ink-stained lines, a life unfolds,
Characters breathe, their tales ignite.
Through whispers of the pen, the bold,
We glimpse their fears, their joys, their fight.

Each chapter spins a world anew,
Where dreams collide with bitter truth.
From heart to heart, the words pursue,
The essence captured, ageless youth.

Silent screams and laughter blend,
In every paragraph, a stake.
With every curve, the stories bend,
And from the stillness, worlds awake.

Together in this crafted space,
We wander through both dark and light.
In portraits drawn with prose's grace,
We find reflections of our plight.

The Lineage of Language

Echoes of ages past arise,
In whispers shared beneath the skies.
Words like rivers carve their way,
Binding hearts in night and day.

Stories told, a dance of sound,
In syllables, our roots are found.
From ancient scripts to modern prose,
In every tongue, a tale that grows.

Emotions woven through each line,
A tapestry of thoughts that shine.
From elders' lore to children's dreams,
In every word, a thread that seams.

Let language flow, a living stream,
With every phrase, we weave and dream.
In this lineage, we find our place,
A shared endeavor, a human grace.

Mapping Meaning

In the stillness, concepts bloom,
Shadows dance, dispelling gloom.
Paths created, each thought a guide,
Through tangled woods, we choose to stride.

Lines of logic, maps unfold,
Every question, a treasure told.
In symbols sharp, we find our way,
Bridges built where ideas sway.

Pixels of thoughts in digital forms,
Carving worlds through quiet storms.
With every click, new lands appear,
A quest for meaning, year by year.

As we wander, charts will change,
Explorers bold in thoughts so strange.
Mapping meaning through time and space,
Charting our souls in a vast embrace.

Refrains of Reality

Time's soft echo fills the air,
Moments captured, stripped of care.
Every heartbeat, a note in tune,
In life's melody, we softly croon.

Stars above blink in reply,
Stories whispered in the sky.
The moon reflects our dreams and fears,
Refrains of joy, of loss, of tears.

Seasons turn with gentle grace,
Life's refrain, a winding race.
In laughter shared or silence felt,
The heart's refrain, forever dealt.

Through every trial, every glee,
Refrains of life define and free.
In every breath, a song that rings,
In reality's chorus, our spirit sings.

Fractals of Feeling

In patterns deep, emotions swirl,
Each moment's pulse, a tender twirl.
Fractals weave through heart and mind,
Reflections of what we seek to find.

Colors burst in vibrant hue,
Layered dreams with each view.
In joy and sorrow, facets glow,
A spectrum vast, a river's flow.

Echoes resonate, a tender call,
In every rise, there's risk of fall.
Yet through each twist, we brave and bend,
In fractals of feeling, we transcend.

As we explore this tangled art,
Each piece connects, a sacred part.
In endless loops of love and pain,
Fractals of feeling, our hearts remain.

Artistry in Arrangement

Colors dance upon the page,
Shapes entwined in a graceful ballet.
Form and function engage,
Crafted dreams on display.

Lines that twist and curves that flow,
Textures whisper soft embrace.
In this canvas, visions grow,
Stories hidden, we explore their space.

A moment caught, a fleeting glance,
Each piece speaks a silent song.
Within this world, we take a chance,
To know where we truly belong.

Harmony in every stroke,
Crafted thoughts take weary flight.
Artistry that words evoke,
Illuminates the darkest night.

Constructs of Contemplation

Thoughts like bricks, stack and align,
Building walls around the mind.
Echoes dance in space divine,
Each reflection, a truth to find.

In stillness, wisdom often speaks,
Quiet moments, deep and clear.
Through the silence, insight leaks,
Perspective shifts, bringing near.

Every corner holds a dream,
Every window, a chance to see.
Softly flows the inner stream,
Where light breaks through, we can be free.

Layered thoughts, a grand design,
Unraveled threads of what we know.
Within this maze, our paths combine,
Constructs of heart, where spirits glow.

Rhythms of Creation

Beats arise from silent seams,
A symphony of heart and hand.
In the stillness, flow the dreams,
Music built upon the land.

Melodies that shape the air,
Dancing shadows in the night.
Creation springs from vibrant care,
As colors burst, taking flight.

Each note found, each word penned,
Crafts a tapestry so bold.
In the rhythm, we transcend,
In the echoes, stories told.

Creation flows like a river's song,
With every breath, a brand new start.
In this dance, we all belong,
Rhythms beating, one shared heart.

Lines Unwritten

Pages bare, a tranquil space,
Ink awaits, a tale untold.
In the silence, dreams embrace,
Every whisper, brave and bold.

Uncharted paths of thought unbound,
Imagine where the stories weave.
Potent truths in silence found,
Moments captured in a sleeve.

Future echoes softly call,
As shadows dance on time's great stage.
In the stillness, we find all,
Lessons carved upon each page.

Lines unwritten, yet to flow,
Promises that time will make.
In the unknown, we will grow,
With every step, the chance we take.

Sculpting Sound Waves

In the quiet of the night,
Whispers dance on the air,
Notes ripple through the stars,
Crafting echoes, free and rare.

Hands tune the unspoken dreams,
Breathing life into the void,
Creating art from silence,
With each wave, we're overjoyed.

Fingers trace the melodies,
Chasing shadows, soft and bright,
Sculpting symphonies in darkness,
Turning whispers into light.

In symphonic harmony,
Every sound finds its own pace,
A universe of music,
Time and space can't erase.

Cantos and Cornices

Under arches of old stone,
Cantos rise like morning dew,
Stories woven with whispers,
In every crevice, truth shines through.

Cornices hold the heavens,
Carvings echo tales of yore,
Voices blend in sacred chorus,
Each note a key, each breath a door.

Beneath the vaulted skies,
Harmony fills the air we share,
In every lyric, a heartbeat,
In every silence, a prayer.

Melodies dance in the breeze,
Carrying dreams on wings of night,
Cantos and cornices unite,
In the glow of the soft moonlight.

Mosaic of Meaning

Pieces fit like gentle thoughts,
Colors blend in quiet grace,
With every shard, a story told,
In the gaps, connection's trace.

Fragments of our lives collide,
A tapestry of joys and woes,
Each hue a reflection of heart,
In the chaos, beauty grows.

Sharpened edges find their place,
In the puzzle, sense unites,
In the depths of each small part,
Lies the essence of our sights.

This mosaic, bold and bright,
Crafted from the past's embrace,
A canvas where we intertwine,
In every bit, a warm trace.

Syntax of the Soul

Words dance with silent pauses,
Constructing meaning that's not seen,
In the syntax of our being,
Each sentence holds what might have been.

Phrases intertwine like rivers,
Flowing through our shared intent,
In the grammar of existence,
Every heartbeat, a testament.

Colloquialisms roll like waves,
Diction painting thoughts refined,
In the lexicon of living,
Every voice with love aligned.

Through the poems of our lives,
Syntax weaves a tale anew,
In the dialogue of our souls,
Truth emerges, clear and true.

Interlacing Ideas

In shadows cast by gentle light,
A tapestry of thoughts takes flight.
Weaving dreams in silent night,
Interlaced, they spark delight.

Whispers of the heart entwine,
In every fold, a secret sign.
Minds connect, the stars align,
In this dance, all paths combine.

From distant shores, we gather near,
Each voice a note, both soft and clear.
Harmony, we hold so dear,
In myriad forms, we persevere.

Through fleeting moments, we create,
A world of wonders, love, and fate.
Together we elevate,
In union, we celebrate.

Threading Through Thought

Thoughts entwined like strands of gold,
Stories waiting to be told.
We journey through the vast unknown,
Woven hearts, we find our home.

Silent musings on the breeze,
Thoughts drift softly through the trees.
In every thread, a tale persists,
A dance of minds, we can't resist.

Moments shared and gently spun,
In tangled webs, we've just begun.
Illuminated by the sun,
Together, we are never done.

Through the labyrinth, we will roam,
Each idea a stepping stone.
In this tapestry we weave,
A universe, we shall believe.

Resounding Resonance

Echoes linger in the air,
Every sound a tale laid bare.
In the silence, whispers play,
Resonance that guides our way.

Through the chambers of our minds,
Harmonies in layers find.
Every note a bridge we cross,
In this dance, we gain, not loss.

Ripples travel far and wide,
A symphony we cannot hide.
Vibrations pulse with every beat,
In unity, we feel complete.

Let the music carry forth,
To the skies, to the earth, to the north.
In resonance, our souls unite,
Together, we embrace the light.

The Canvas of Poetics

On a canvas stretched and wide,
Words like colors, they collide.
Brushstrokes of the heart and mind,
In this art, true peace we find.

Each stanza paints a vivid scene,
Emotions flow, both raw and keen.
In every line, a brush of grace,
Capturing time, a sacred space.

With ink and dreams, we craft the tale,
In whispers soft, we set our sail.
Through the storms and gentle winds,
The canvas grows as life begins.

Upon this stage, our spirits soar,
Creating worlds to explore.
In the blend of dark and light,
We find our truth, we find our sight.

Schemes and Dreams

In the quiet night, we plot our ways,
Hopes entwined in the silver rays.
Dreams take flight on whispered threads,
Schemes like stars fill our heads.

Paths unfold like petals bright,
Guided by the moon's soft light.
Each heartbeat dances, aligned with fate,
In this moment, we create our state.

Colors splash on canvases wide,
Imagination flows, a flowing tide.
The world spins with our heart's embrace,
In schemes and dreams, we find our place.

Futures beckon, shadows fade,
In every risk, a chance is laid.
With every step, the world we weave,
In schemes and dreams, we shall believe.

Balancing Beats

Rhythms echo in the depths of night,
Every heartbeat, a flickering light.
Step by step, we move with grace,
Balancing beats in life's embrace.

Time flows like a river wide,
Moments merge and coincide.
With every pause, a truth unfolds,
In the silence, the heart beholds.

Voices blend, a symphony starts,
Melodies twine with our beating hearts.
In the dance, we find our way,
Balancing beats in night and day.

Harmony whispers in every breath,
A balance achieved, defying death.
Life's tempo sways, yet remains sweet,
In every heartbeat, we find our beat.

Patterns in Breath

Inhale deep, the world attunes,
Exhale softly, chasing moons.
Patterns form like gentle waves,
In the stillness, the spirit braves.

Each breath a mark, a fleeting trace,
In the rhythm, we find our space.
Connected threads weave through the air,
Patterns pulse, beyond compare.

Like whispers of the trees that sway,
Breath holds secrets of night and day.
In this dance, the heart reveals,
Patterns in breath, the soul heals.

Awake to life, and start to feel,
In every breath, a chance to heal.
Among the patterns, softly tread,
In the sacred space, where dreams are bred.

The Edifice of Emotion

Walls stand tall, built on dreams,
A fortress fashioned from heartfelt beams.
Each brick laid with care and strife,
The edifice of emotion, our life.

Windows wide, letting light seep,
Through laughter shared and secrets deep.
Every room holds memories dear,
In the edifice, love draws near.

Foundations strong, like tender trust,
In storms we stand, as we must.
Through cracks and crevices, lessons flow,
The edifice of emotion continues to grow.

In every corner, echoes linger,
Touching the heart with a gentle finger.
We build with stories, hopes, and pain,
In this structure, we choose to remain.

Dances of Diction

Words twirl in the air,
Ballet of thoughts, a vibrant affair.
Silence speaks when hearts unite,
In whispers soft, they take flight.

Each phrase a step, each glance a pause,
Chasing shadows, breaking laws.
Rhythms blend in a sweet embrace,
The dance of words leaves no trace.

From sonnets deep to laughter's cheer,
Every syllable draws us near.
A tapestry woven, bright and bold,
In diction's dance, stories unfold.

Echoes linger, the night grows long,
In the silent spaces, the unsung song.
With every dance, a tale begins,
Dances of diction, where love wins.

Patterns of Passion

Hearts entwined in a vivid thread,
Every color, a word unsaid.
Whispers dance upon the skin,
In patterns bright, desire spins.

Velvet nights with starlit sighs,
Passion's palette, love never lies.
In every touch, a story told,
Patterns of passion, fierce and bold.

Moments flicker, like candlelight,
Drawn together, lost in the night.
The patterns shift with every kiss,
A map of longing, purest bliss.

As dawn breaks with its golden hue,
We trace the paths of me and you.
In the silence, hearts still throng,
Patterns of passion, forever strong.

Grids of Imagery

Canvas laid with hues of dreams,
Each brushstroke flows, or so it seems.
Lines intersect in vibrant flow,
Grids of imagery, a visual show.

Layers build with every thought,
Fragments of worlds, beautifully caught.
Shapes unfold in a dance so free,
Visions emerge, as we can see.

Mountains rise from valleys deep,
In the quiet, secrets keep.
Textures breathe through the painted air,
Grids of imagery, rich and rare.

In the stillness, colors speak,
Tales of wonder, never bleak.
With every glance, our spirits grow,
In grids of imagery, we flow.

The Blueprint of Meaning

Lines drawn on pages bare,
Sketching thoughts with gentle care.
Blueprints form as ideas flow,
In the silence, insights grow.

Foundations laid with steady hands,
Constructing dreams upon the sands.
Every detail, a thought divine,
The blueprint of meaning, yours and mine.

Walls of wisdom rise so tall,
Echoing truth, inviting all.
With every brick, a lesson learned,
In this journey, our hearts burned.

As visions merge in pastel light,
We chart our course through day and night.
The structure solid, yet so lean,
In the blueprint of meaning, we glean.

Pillars of Poetry

In shadows cast by words that flow,
Sturdy pillars begin to grow.
Each line a stone, carefully placed,
A structure of thoughts, interlaced.

Whispers travel, strong and light,
Under the moon, through day and night.
Verses standing, bold and proud,
Echoes dance within the crowd.

Crafted lines that rise and fall,
In silence, they answer the call.
Filling spaces, forming grace,
In this realm, they find their place.

Unseen hands that shape the air,
Where dreams and words both dare to share.
Pillars strong, they hold the light,
In this fortress, hearts take flight.

Lattice of Lyrics

A lattice formed of tangled thought,
Each lyric crafted, carefully wrought.
Interwoven, they twist and bend,
In symphony, they softly blend.

Notes that rise like morning dew,
Painting skies in shades anew.
Harmonies that kiss the breeze,
With melodies that aim to please.

Rhythms pulse in every heart,
From silence, the verses start.
A structure built with tender care,
Each word a thread, spun from air.

In this garden, seeds are sown,
Where lyrics bloom, and dreams are grown.
Together they form a living art,
A lattice of lyrics, touching the heart.

Versed in Form

Versed in form, with rules to keep,
Each stanza crafted from silent deep.
Lines align in structured grace,
Finding rhythm, a steady pace.

Meter guides the writer's hand,
Building bridges, a thoughtful strand.
Rhyme entwined in dance so sweet,
Creating harmony in each beat.

Each verse a journey, step by step,
In harmony, the heart is kept.
Forms may vary, yet truth remains,
In patterned words, the soul sustains.

A dance of phrases, bright and bold,
Timeless stories begin to unfold.
Versed in form, we find our way,
In lines of light, we greet the day.

Echoes of Arrangement

In echoes of arrangement, we find,
The harmony of heart and mind.
Phrases linger, soft and clear,
Like whispered thoughts that draw us near.

Each echo carries weight and grace,
Tracing paths in boundless space.
Arranged as flowers, fresh and bright,
In every corner, light ignites.

The power of words, elegantly cast,
Resonates through ages past.
Structured beauty, woven tight,
In echoes, we discover light.

Expressions shaped by hands unseen,
Creating worlds in vivid sheen.
In every echo, stories bloom,
A tapestry, dispelling gloom.

Symmetry in Syllables

In whispers soft, the words align,
Each beat a note, in perfect time.
A rhythm found in gentle flow,
Where silence speaks and feelings grow.

With every glance, a tale unfolds,
A dance of thoughts, both young and old.
The structure sings, a subtle cue,
In harmony, we find what's true.

Each syllable a stepping stone,
A pathway carved, yet never known.
With balance tucked in every line,
A symmetry that feels divine.

We breathe the air of crafted verse,
A world of wonder, not a curse.
In simple terms, we intertwine,
Creating magic, pure design.

Chords of Language

In sounds that ring and softly blend,
Langauge flows, a daring trend.
Each word a chord, a vibrant hue,
A symphony where hearts break through.

From simple talks, grand tales arise,
With treble high and bass that sighs.
Exploring dreams, so vast and wide,
Together, we take the same ride.

Melodies in every phrase,
Crafting moments, passion ablaze.
With echoes sweet in shared delight,
We paint the world, both day and night.

In every voice, a story sings,
Connected through the love it brings.
The chords of language, woven tight,
Create a canvas, pure and bright.

The Balance of Lines

In verses strung like pearls on thread,
Each line a thought, to be spread.
A measured pace, a steady beat,
Where mind and soul in balance meet.

The weight of meaning shifts and sways,
In crafted lines, the heart's own ways.
A push and pull, like tides at sea,
In each new stanza, we are free.

The structure holds, yet bends with grace,
An artful dance, a slow embrace.
In journeys marked by ink and light,
We chart our dreams into the night.

The balance strikes, a perfect tie,
To lift the spirit, let it fly.
In simple terms, we find our place,
In every line, a warm embrace.

Harmonizing the Heart

Beneath the stars, the feelings stir,
In gentle tones, the heart's purr.
With every beat, we sing as one,
A tale of love, a life begun.

The whispers shared in twilight's glow,
A melody that ebbs and flows.
We find our voice, both strong and clear,
In harmony, we hold what's dear.

With every glance, our spirits soar,
A warmth that binds, forevermore.
In synchronized, we learn to stand,
Two souls entwined, hand in hand.

The music plays beneath the moon,
In secrets shared, we find our tune.
To harmonize, to feel, to dare,
Is to be lost, and still, be there.

Harmonious Constructs

In twilight's glow, the whispers play,
A symphony of night and day.
Each note a brush upon the sky,
As dreams and hopes begin to fly.

The stars align in gentle tune,
While hearts embrace the silver moon.
Together, they weave a tapestry,
Of love, of laughter, and mystery.

A world constructed in soft hues,
Where every shade is meant to fuse.
In colors bright and shadows deep,
Awake the wonders that we keep.

With every breath, a story told,
In rhythms warm, both brave and bold.
Here in this space, we find our song,
A place where all our dreams belong.

Verses as Vessels

Each verse a ship on ocean's vast,
Sailing forth, horizons cast.
With ink as wind to guide the way,
Our thoughts set sail at break of day.

The waves of words, they rise and swell,
In every line, a tale to tell.
Verse by verse, we weave the thread,
Bringing whispers from the dead.

In stanzas formed, connections bloom,
Filling the air with fragrant plume.
These vessels hold our fears and cheer,
The echoes of what's precious here.

Through endless seas of thought and ink,
We navigate and pause to think.
With every phrase, a journey's begun,
In words, we seek our unison.

Portraits in Poetic Form

Each poem crafted like a frame,
A captured smile, a whispered name.
In stanzas bright, we paint our views,
With colors bold, we dare to choose.

A portrait not of ink alone,
But of the heart, a flesh and bone.
In every word a life unfolds,
A tapestry of dreams and gold.

Brush strokes made of rhythm and rhyme,
In moments fleeting, frozen time.
To showcase love, to mark the pain,
Each verse a window to regain.

In this gallery of soul and thought,
Every piece a battle fought.
A mirror held to lives we live,
In artful layers, we forgive.

Choreography of Words

In elegant lines, the dancers sway,
Words pirouette in bright array.
Their rhythms pulse, a heartbeat's song,
As stanzas weave where we belong.

With every verse, a step unfolds,
A story shared, a truth retold.
The movement flows, both fierce and light,
With whispers soft, igniting night.

Across the stage, our thoughts entwined,
In every leap, new worlds we find.
An ardent dance of passion's fire,
Each line a spark, each word a choir.

In synchrony, the voices rise,
A ballet drawn from earth and skies.
We join the dance, our spirits soar,
In this choreography, we explore.

Milton Keynes UK
Ingram Content Group UK Ltd.
UKHW020704191024
449793UK00005B/44